HALLOWEEN SPOOKY MOSAIC COLOR BY NUMBER COLORING BOOK

CURATED FRAMES PUBLISHING

Published by Curated Frames Ltd

info@curatedframespublishing.com

Cover design by

Illustrations by Curated Frames Publishing

Scan to join our mailing list and receive five free designs.

WELCOME

Welcome to a spooktacular adventure filled with haunting colors, eerie creativity, and bone-chilling tranquility, all nestled within the pages of our Halloween Spooky Mosaic Color by Number Coloring Book, designed for little ghouls and goblins aged 5 and up. Venture into the bewitching domain of nocturnal creatures and haunted spirits, where intricate patterns and spine-tingling mosaic designs conjure a labyrinth of calming chills and spellbinding artistry.

SHARE

Start a ripple of creativity! Share your unique artwork and experiences from our Halloween Spooky Mosaic Spectacular Color by Number Coloring Book. Follow us and post your creations on Instagram. Make sure to use the hashtag **#ultimatecoloringbooks** to inspire others and have the opportunity to be featured on our platforms.

JOIN

Become an exclusive member of our creative community! Sign up for our mailing list and receive five additional coloring pages absolutely free as a welcome gift. By joining, you'll get updates on new releases, special offers, coloring tips, and a lot more. Your artistic journey is worth celebrating, and we'd love to be part of it.

Get access to poster sized versions of your favourite designs.

Scan the code below

GHASTLY GHOST

Guide Remap

Black

Dark Brown

Chestnut Brown

Mocha

Dark Slate Gray

Sienna

Taupe

Burnt Orange

Pumpkin Orange

Tangerine

Mango

Beige

Cream

	1
	2
	3
	4
	5
	6
	7
	8
	9
	10
	11
	12
	13

Interesting fact:
Ghosts can sometimes be heard but not seen. Ghosts can sometimes move objects. They are often depicted as being able to walk through walls.

Mosaic Halloween Ghoul Spectacular

WICKED WITCH

Guide	Remap
Pitch Black	1
Deep Forest Green	2
Dark Chestnut	3
Dark Mocha	4
Rusty Brown	5
Burnt Sienna	6
Light Taupe	7
Bright Orange	8
Carrot Orange	9
Caramel	10
Tangerine	11
Apricot	12
Peach	13
Sandy Brown	14
Light Peach	15
Pale Beige	16

Interesting fact:
Witches often use cauldrons for their potions. The "Witching Hour" is considered to be midnight. Witches are often associated with black cats.

Mosaic Halloween Ghoul Spectacular

THE HUNGRY VAMPIRE

Guide	Remap
White	1
Ivory	2
Ecru	3
Sand	4
Khaki	5
Tan	6
Grayish Brown	7
Dark Taupe	8
Bright Red	9
Dark Red	10
Dark Olive	11
Ebony	12
Dark Maroon	13
Very Dark Brown	14
Charcoal	15
Black	16

Interesting fact:

Vampires are often shown transforming into bats.

The most famous vampire is Count Dracula from Bram Stoker's novel.

Mosaic Halloween Ghoul Spectacular

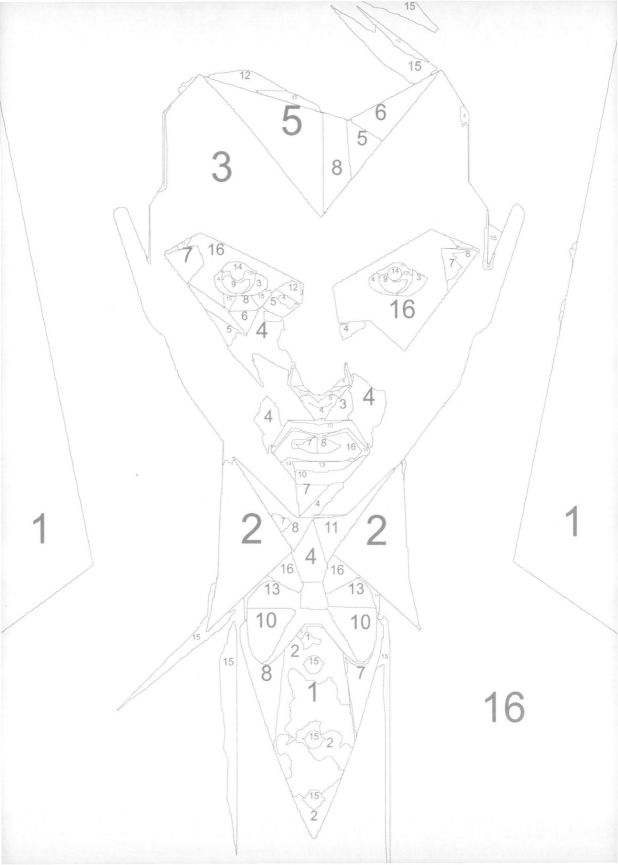

WHO'S YOUR MUMMY!

Guide   Remap

Near Black		1
Charcoal		2
Dark Slate Gray		3
Rust		4
Dark Mustard		5
Vermilion		6
Copper		7
Slate Gray		8
Bronze		9
Warm Gray		10
Light Taupe		11
Pale Gold		12
Beige		13
Bone		14
Off-White		15
Ivory		16

Interesting fact:
Mummies have been found on every continent. They are commonly associated with ancient Egypt.

Mosaic Halloween Ghoul Spectacular

WEREWOLF

	Guide	Remap
Black		1
Midnight Blue		2
Espresso		3
Dark Brown		4
Maroon		5
Teal		6
Brick Red		7
Bright Red		8
Steel Blue		9
Light Steel Blue		10
Sky Blue		11
Bright Yellow		12
Pale Yellow		13
Powder Blue		14
Pastel Yellow		15
Eggshell		16

Interesting fact:
Werewolves transform from humans into wolves during a full moon. They are often depicted as strong and fast. Lycanthropy is the term for the transformation process.

Mosaic Halloween Ghoul Spectacular

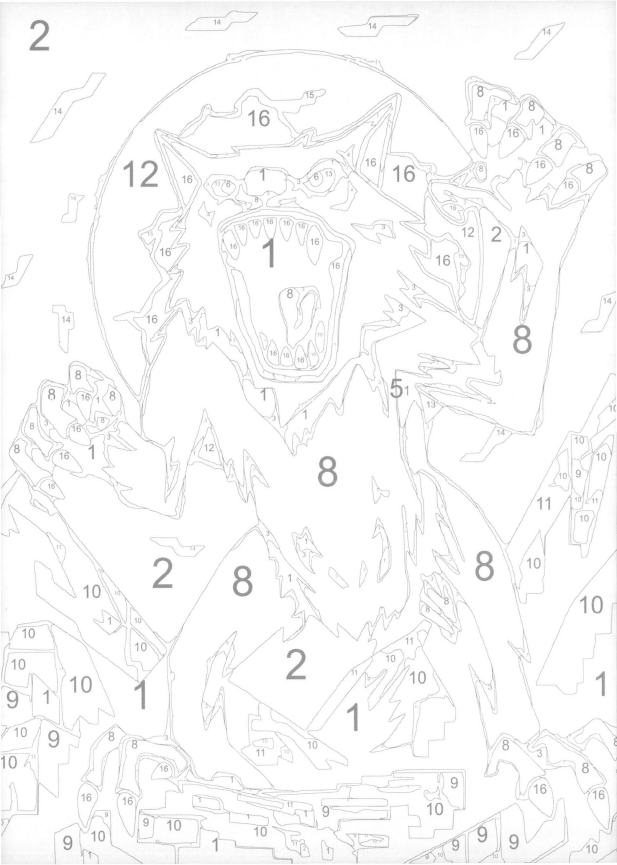

FRANKENSTEIN'S MONSTER

	Guide	Remap
Light Gray		1
Lime Green		2
Taupe Gray		3
Gray		4
Sage Green		5
Bright Green		6
Kelly Green		7
Orange		8
Medium Green		9
Dark Orange		10
Red-Orange		11
Charcoal Gray		12
Almost Black		13
Black		14
Very Dark Green		15
Pitch Black		16

Interesting fact:
Created by Mary Shelley in her novel "Frankenstein. He is brought to life through electricity. Often misunderstood and seeks companionship.

SKELETON

	Guide	Remap
White		1
Light Gray		2
Warm Gray		3
Yellow		4
Light Brown		5
Gray		6
Pumpkin Orange		7
Dark Orange		8
Brick Red		9
Olive		10
Charcoal		11
Rust		12
Charcoal		13
Black		14
Black		15
		16

Interesting fact:
They are popular decorations during Halloween. Skeletons are often depicted as dancing or playing music.

Mosaic Halloween Ghoul Spectacular

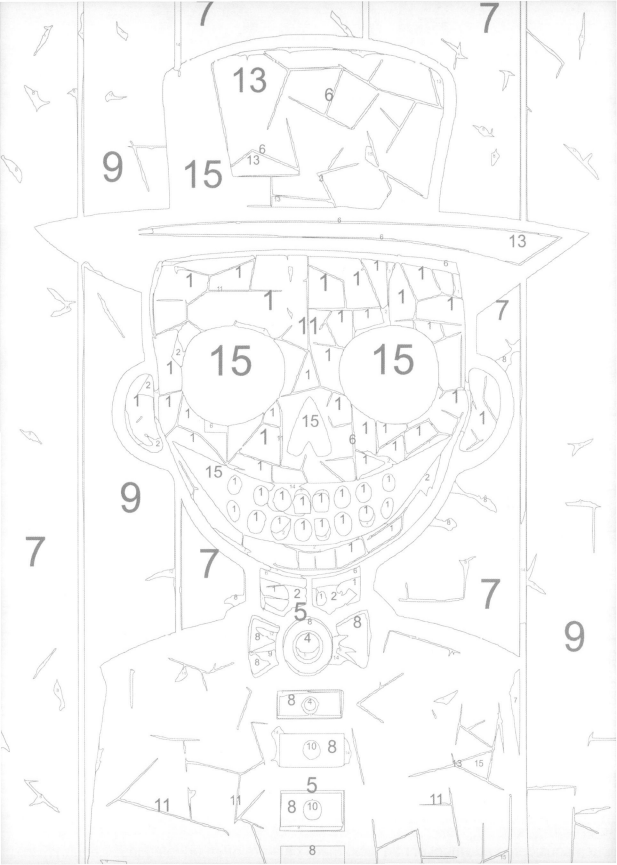

BLACK CAT

	Guide	Remap
Near Black		1
Dark Gray		2
Brick Red		3
Medium Gray		4
Bright Red		5
Slate Gray		6
Bright Orange		7
Royal Blue		8
Steel Blue		9
Bronze		10
Stone Gray		11
Bright Yellow		12
Gold		13
Beige		14
Light Beige		15
Ivory		16

Interesting fact:
Often considered a symbol of bad luck. Black cats are often adopted less frequently than other cats.

BAT

Guide	Remap
Black	1
Charcoal	2
Brick Red	3
Slate Gray	4
Tomato Red	5
Steel Gray	6
Bright Orange	7
Cobalt Blue	8
Cadet Blue	9
Tawny	10
Stone Gray	11
Sunflower Yellow	12
Goldenrod	13
Wheat	14
Pale Beige	15
Cream	16

Interesting fact:
Bats are the only mammals capable of sustained flight. Often associated with vampires.

PUMPKIN

	Guide	Remap
Near Black		1
Dark Brown		2
Sienna		3
Plum		4
Forest Green		5
Rust		6
Taupe Gray		7
Olive Green		8
Burnt Orange		9
Slate Gray		10
Tangerine		11
Mango		12
Sage Green		13
Mustard Yellow		14
Sea foam Green		15
White		16

Interesting fact:
Popular in folklore as a symbol of the harvest. Sometimes considered a guardian of the fields.

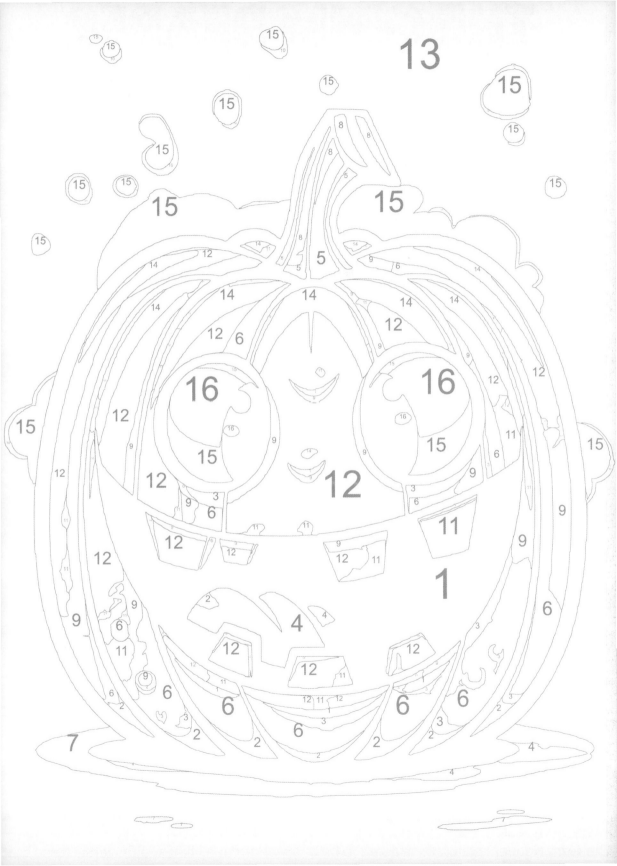

THE GRIM REAPER

Guide	Remap

Near Black

Dark Brown

Charcoal

Mahogany

Sienna

Olive Drab

Copper

Medium Gray

Burnt Orange

Bright Orange

Khaki

Tangerine

Light Taupe

Apricot

Beige

Interesting fact:
The Grim Reaper is often considered to be everywhere at all times, a universal force that no one can escape. You might see the Grim Reaper in stories or cartoons, where he's often shown as someone who reminds people to be careful and make good choices.

Mosaic Halloween Ghoul Spectacular

GOBLIN

	Guide	Remap
Black		1
Dark Olive Green		2
Mahogany		3
Green		4
Dark Slate Gray		5
Rust		6
Olive		7
Gray		8
Burnt Orange		9
Lime Green		10
Chartreuse		11
Amber		12
Sandy Brown		13
Yellow Green		14
Pale Green		15
Off-White		16

Goblins are known for being mischievous and sneaky. They love playing tricks on people, but they're usually more naughty than truly evil.

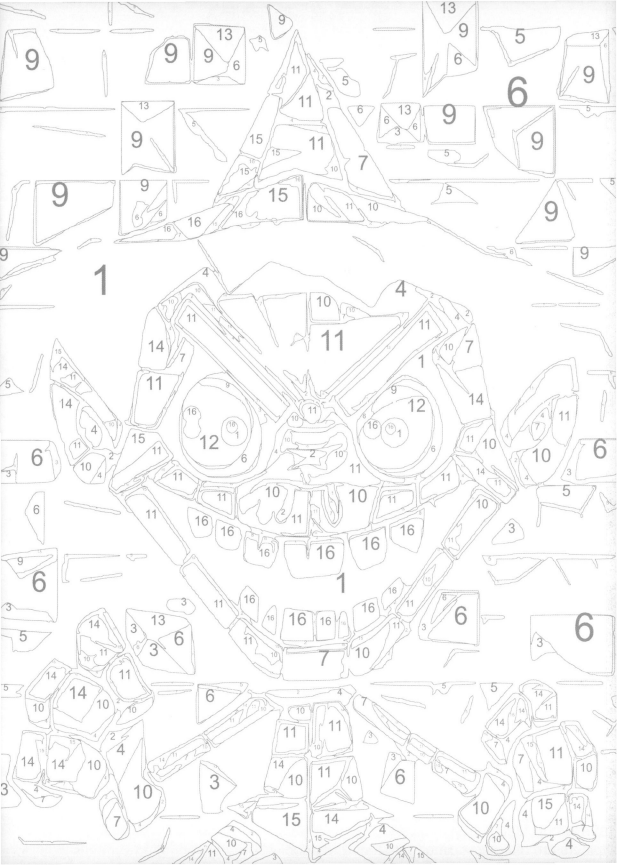

SPIDER

Color	Guide	Remap
Black		1
Dark Olive		2
Dark Brown		3
Deep Red		4
Olive Drab		5
Bronze		6
Brick Red		7
Tan		8
Amber		9
Light Brown		10
Golden Brown		11
Beige		12
Slate Gray		13
Peach		14
Pale Beige		15
Ivory		16

Interesting fact:
Spiders are often associated with fear and phobias.They are common symbols in folklore for patience and creativity.Spiders produce silk to create webs.Some spiders are venomous.

SCARECROW

White

Silver

Bright Yellow

Gold

Grayish Green

Tangerine

Pumpkin Orange

Bronze

Burnt Orange

Dark Tan

Sienna

Rust

Mahogany

Dark Olive

Espresso

Black

1
2
3
4
5
6
7
8
9
10
11
12
13
14
15
16

Interesting fact:
They are often depicted as human-like figures made of straw. Scarecrows are popular in folklore as guardians of the field. They are a common symbol of the harvest season.

SPOOKY DOLL

	Guide	Remap
Near Black		1
Dark Brown		2
Charcoal		3
Taupe		4
Sienna		5
Grayish Brown		6
Copper		7
Burnt Orange		8
Bronze		9
Bright Orange		10
Warm Gray		11
Tangerine		12
Pumpkin Orange		13
Light Taupe		14
Light Beige		15
Ivory		16

Interesting fact:
People are really interested in haunted dolls, and you can see them talked about a lot on social media, in movies, and even in special studies. They're spookily popular.

Mosaic Halloween Ghoul Spectacular

THE HAUNTED HOUSE

Guide	Remap	
Near Black		1
Dark Forest Green		2
Mahogany		3
Slate Gray		4
Teal Green		5
Brick Red		6
Sea Green		7
Taupe Gray		8
Bright Orange		9
Steel Blue		10
Tangerine		11
Light Teal		12
Mustard Yellow		13
Light Gray		14
Pale Yellow		15
Eggshell		16

Interesting fact:
A building said to be inhabited by ghosts or spirits.A popular theme for Halloween parties and events.Often features creaky doors, cobwebs, and eerie sounds.

Mosaic Halloween Ghoul Spectacular

FULL MOON

	Guide	Remap
Black		1
Charcoal		2
Mahogany		3
Dark Taupe		4
Dark Brown		5
Brick Red		6
Bright Red		7
Grayish Brown		8
Burnt Orange		9
Terra Cotta		10
Warm Gray		11
Tangerine		12
Sandy Brown		13
Wheat		14
Light Beige		15
Ivory		16

Interesting fact:
A moon that is fully illuminated, often associated with werewolves. A common backdrop in Halloween scenes. symbolizes mystery and the unknown.

Mosaic Halloween Ghoul Spectacular

SWAMP MONSTER

	Guide	Remap
Black		1
Dark Olive Green		2
Olive Drab		3
Dark Mustard		4
Forest Green		5
Teal Green		6
Moss Green		7
Bronze		8
Olive		9
Amber		10
Lime Green		11
Chartreuse		12
Sage Green		13
Pale Yellow		14
Seafoam Green		15
Off-White		16

Interesting fact:
They are popular in horror films and literature. Swamp Monsters are often shown as being covered in algae or mud.

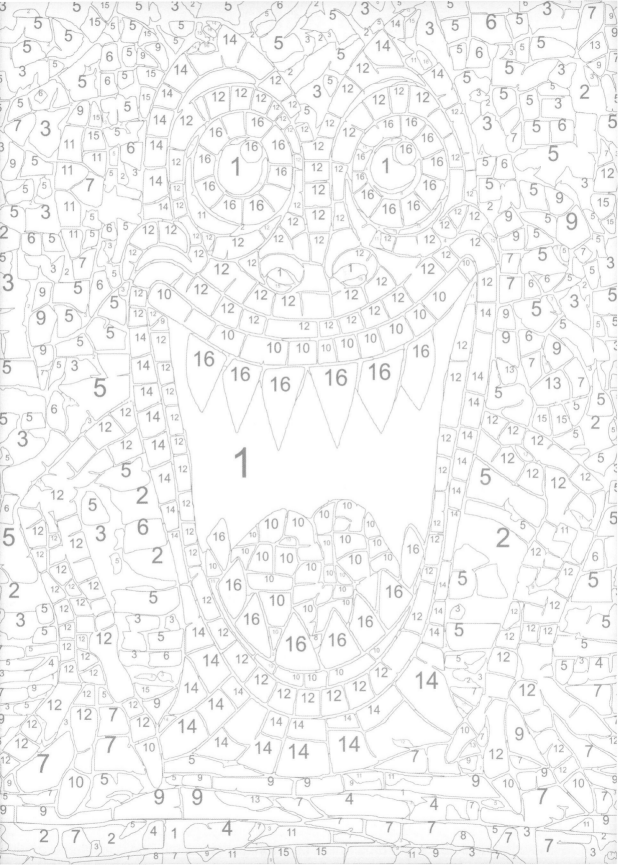

THE DEVIL

	Guide	Remap
Near Black		1
Dark Red		2
Charcoal		3
Maroon		4
Brick Red		5
Bright Red		6
Fire Engine Red		7
Terra Cotta		8
Tomato Red		9
Warm Gray		10
Coral		11
Salmon		12
Light Gray		13
Silver		14
Off-White		15

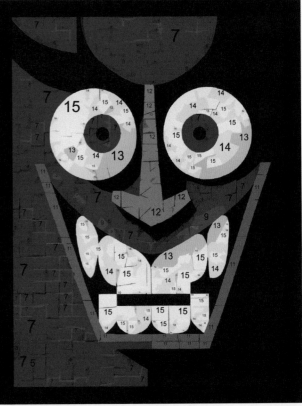

Interesting fact:
The Devil is often depicted with horns and a pitchfork. He is sometimes considered a fallen angel.

Mosaic Halloween Ghoul Spectacular

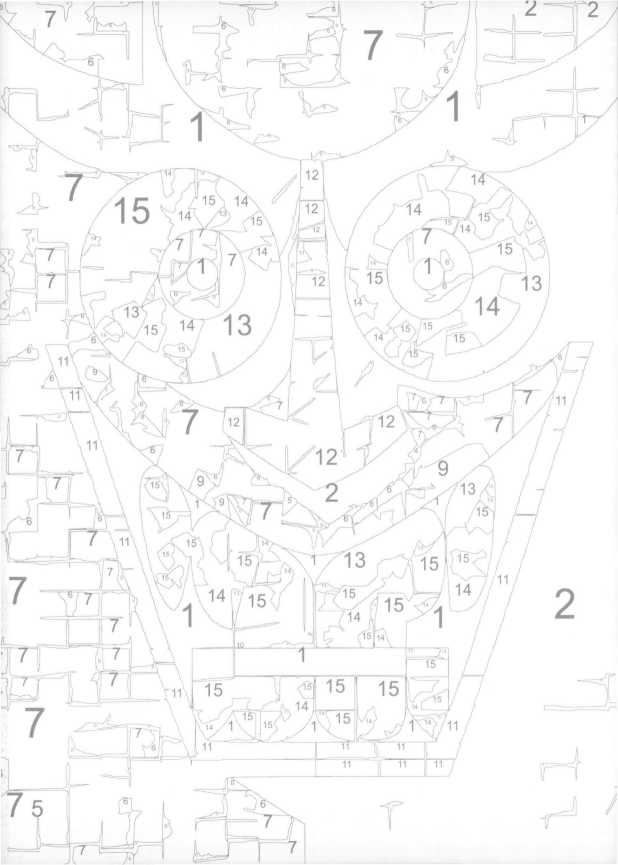

ALIEN

	Guide	Remap
Dark Olive		1
Dark Brown		2
Dark Slate Gray		3
Mustard Brown		4
Forest Green		5
Bright Orange		6
Bronze		7
Lime Green		8
Tangerine		9
Chartreuse		10
Sage Green		11
Gold		12
Sunflower Yellow		13
Light Green		14
Pale Green		15
White		16

Interesting fact:
Aliens are often shown as advanced and technologically superior.UFO sightings are often associated with aliens.The Roswell incident is a famous alleged alien encounter.

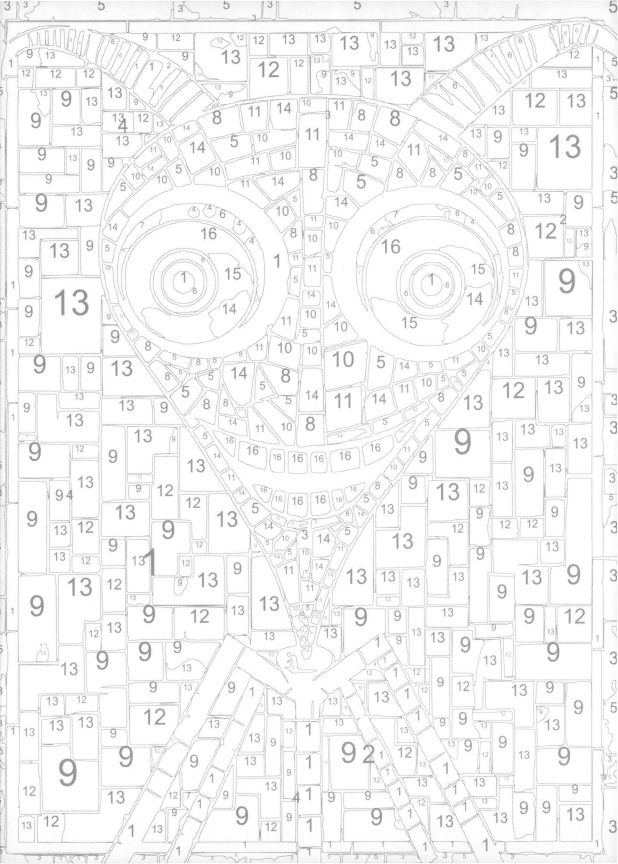

BUCKET OF TREATS

Guide	Remap
Black	1
Chestnut	2
Teal Blue	3
Crimson	4
Bright Red	5
Copper	6
Kelly Green	7
Turquoise	8
Burnt Orange	9
Tan	10
Slate Blue	11
Amber	12
Coral	13
Wheat	14
Light Blue	15
Ivory	16

Interesting fact:
Everyone loves sweets!

HAY BALES

Guide	Remap

Near Black 1

Dark Brown 2

Sienna 3

Taupe 4

Bronze 5

Warm Gray 6

Burnt Orange 7

Pumpkin Orange 8

Tangerine 9

Light Brown 10

Bright Orange 11

Beige 12

Sandy Brown 13

Light Beige 14

Peach 15

Eggshell 16

Interesting fact:

Mosaic Halloween Ghoul Spectacular

THE GOOD ANGEL

Guide	Remap
Dark Brown	1
Chestnut	2
Bright Red	3
Olive Drab	4
Copper	5
Slate Gray	6
Pumpkin Orange	7
Tan	8
Cadet Blue	9
Wheat	10
Sunflower Yellow	11
Pale Gold	12
Light Teal	13
Light Beige	14
Pale Green	15
	16

Interesting fact:
 For many, the angel costume symbolizes goodness and light amidst the darker, spookier themes of Halloween.

HALLOWEEN BUNTING

Guide Remap

Near Black

Dark Olive

Dark Green

Sienna

Dark Taupe

Brick Red

Bronze

Terra Cotta

Warm Gray

Amber

Tangerine

Beige

Light Brown

Pale Beige

Ivory

Interesting fact:
Did you know that Halloween bunting can be like a treasure map for trick-or-treaters? Some families hang special bunting to guide kids to the best spots for treats in their yard or home. It's like following a colorful, spooky trail to candy treasure!

Mosaic Halloween Ghoul Spectacular

CRYSTAL BALL

Guide Remap

Color	Number
Dark Olive	1
Plum Gray	2
Brick Red	3
Dusty Rose	4
Steel Blue	5
Copper	6
Rosewood	7
Slate Gray	8
Sky Blue	9
Tan	10
Mint Green	11
Peach	12
Light Beige	13
Pale Orange	14
Eggshell	15
Off-White	16

Interesting fact:
In stories and movies, crystal balls are often used by wizards, witches, and fortune-tellers to see the future or faraway places. During Halloween, a crystal ball can be a spooky and fun decoration. Some even have lights inside that change colors!

Mosaic Halloween Ghoul Spectacular

Scan for framed color by number prints of your favorite designs. For you or as an amazing gift.

@CURATEDFRAMESPUBLISHING

Scan and join our Instagram our community.

Scan to join our mailing list and receive five free designs.

Dear valued artist,

We wanted to take a moment to express our sincere gratitude for choosing **Halloween Spooky Mosaic Color by Number Coloring Book**. We hope that it has provided you with a source of relaxation, creativity, and joy.

We truly appreciate you embarking on this vibrant journey with us. Now that you've experienced the magic of our **Halloween Spooky Mosaic Color by Number Coloring Book**, we'd love for you to share your colorful masterpieces and experiences with our growing community. Follow us on Instagram, Facebook, and Twitter @UltimateColoringbooks and use the hashtag #halloweenmosaic when you post your artwork. Not only will you inspire others with your creativity, but you'll also get the chance to see how other colorists around the world are bringing their Halloween designs to life. Plus, we regularly feature our favourite works on our social media platforms, so don't miss the chance to showcase your unique creations! Together, let's spread the joy and relaxation that coloring brings, one masterpiece at a time.

Thank you again for choosing our

Halloween Mosaic Color by Number Coloring Book

Printed in Poland
by Amazon Fulfillment
Poland Sp. z o.o., Wrocław

25521764R00031